Following Jesus

3V Bible Studies

Robin H. Kimbrough

Following Jesus

04 05 06 07 08 09 10 11 12 13—10 9 8 7 6 5 4 3 2 1

MANUFACTURED IN THE UNITED STATES OF AMERICA

CONTENTS

3V
Bible
Studies

following Jesus

This Bible study focuses on three key tools for exciting Bible study: comprehension, interpretation, and application.

About
3V Bible Studies

What's the Text? begins by simply reading the Scripture passage for what it says. Then it invites deeper understanding by having us examine and ask questions about the text.

What's the Context? looks at both the literary issues and the cultural and social situation. The information in this section may address specific terms used in the passage, the character of the particular book of the Bible, what comes before the passage, what comes after it, and the events and cultural expectations of the times. Having this "story behind the story" provides important information for understanding the text and its meaning.

What's Next?, the third section, recognizes that studying the Bible is not focused on information, but on transformation. Here's where we intentionally focus on today by looking at different "Views" that relate to contemporary life.

One reason for doing Bible study this way is to learn *how* to study the Bible. As your group works through text, context, and what's next, you will be learning an important skill for a lifetime of encountering God's Word.

The real joy in engaging this Living Word is its power to change our lives—for the better. You don't have to get "right" answers; you do have to be open and searching—and the Spirit will lead you.

Visit www.ileadyouth.com/3V for

◦ student-leader helps
◦ background on the Gospels
◦ worship suggestions
◦ contents of the other studies in the 3V series

Leading the Studies

Adult and Student Leaders

Adults or high school students can lead or co-lead these studies. Interested students can facilitate the whole study or lead a particular discussion or activity for their peers. By using small groups at particular points, all students will gain more experience as both leaders and participants.

Students who have been student-leaders for *Synago* are especially qualified to lead all or portions of these 3V Bible Studies. Go to *www.ileadyouth.com* for student-leader helps and for more information about *Synago* for senior highs.

Activities

As you lead, don't hesitate to try some of the more active ideas (roleplay or drawing, for example). Sometimes the physical and verbal cues of a one-minute roleplay lead to great new insights. Another reason to try the activities is that different people learn in different ways. So expand the opportunities for everyone to learn.

Group Size

All size groups of senior highs can easily use this study method. If your group is small, do most of the sections together, with occasional conversations in pairs or threes. If the group is larger, break into small groups or pairs more often, with times of reporting and talking as a whole group.

Bibles

Everyone should have access to a study book and a Bible. Have a variety of translations of the Bible available. Referring to the different translations is a helpful skill in Bible study. Sometimes subtle nuances in the wording can give more clarity or insight. Sometimes they help raise good questions.

The New Revised Standard Version (NRSV) is printed here so that students can feel good about writing in their books. They can highlight words and phrases they think are important or note questions that the Scripture passage raises for them, which they might not do in a Bible.

Following Jesus

Fitting Your Time

This approach to Bible study is very flexible. You may choose to:

- **Do all of a particular study or streamline it;**
- **Do the study in one session or over two or three;**
- **Do all the questions, or choose some;**
- **Do some of the studies or all of them.**

If you need to spend less time, plan to do What's the Text? and What's the Context? You may wish to deal with fewer of the questions in each section. Be sure to do After Looking at Both the Text and the Context.

If you have more time, add View You in What's Next? If you have still more time, use one or all of the other Views (A, B, C) for some spirited debate.

Suggested Schedule Options

One Session Only

5–10 minutes	What's the Text?
20–25	What's the Context? (Selected Questions)
20–35	What's Next? (Selected Views)
5–10	View You

Two Sessions

10–15 minutes	What's the Text?
20–30	What's the Context? (Selected Questions)
10–15	What's Next (One View)
10–15 minutes	Review of Text and Context
30–40	What's Next? (Remaining Views)
5–10	View You and Worship Suggestions from *www.ileadyouth.com*

Three Sessions

1. Do What's the Text? and What's the Context? (Most Questions)
2. Do a review of Text and Context; finish any remaining Context sections and After Looking at Both the Text and the Context.
3. Do a brief review of previous sessions; choose one or more of the Views in What's Next? Close with View You and Worship Suggestions from *www.ileadyouth.com*.

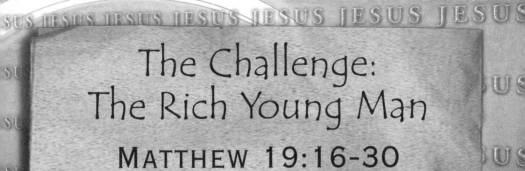

The Challenge:
The Rich Young Man
MATTHEW 19:16-30

You've heard coaches use the expression "Give 110 percent." Maybe a coach has asked you to give that much. It's not easy. You can work hard, playing well, and still the coach wants more. Yet the best players and teams seem to find a way to dig down within themselves to give more.

Coaches didn't invent the call to give 110 percent. Nearly 2,000 years ago, Jesus issued that very challenge to a young man who had it all.

2

16 Then someone came to him and said, "Teacher, what good deed must I do to have eternal life?" 17 And he said to him, "Why do you ask me about what is good? There is only one who is good. If you wish to enter into life, keep the commandments." 18 He said to him, "Which ones?" And Jesus said, "You shall not murder; You shall not commit adultery; You shall not steal; You shall not bear false witness; 19 Honor your father and mother; also, You shall love your neighbor as yourself." 20 The young man said to him, "I have kept all these; what do I still lack?" 21 Jesus said to him, "If you wish to be perfect, go, sell your possessions and give the money to the poor, and you will have treasure in heaven; then come, follow me." 22 When the young man heard this word, he went away grieving, for he had many possessions.

23 Then Jesus said to his disciples, "Truly, I tell you, it will be hard for a rich person to enter the kingdom of heaven. 24 Again I tell you, it is easier for a camel to go through the eye of a needle than for someone who is rich to enter the kingdom of God." 25 When the disciples heard this, they were greatly astounded, and said, "Then who can be saved?" 26 But Jesus looked at them and said, "For mortals it is impossible, but for God all things are possible."

27 Then Peter said in reply, "Look, we have left everything and followed you. What then will we have?" 28 Jesus said to them, "Truly I tell you, at the renewal of all things, when the Son of Man is seated on his throne of his glory, you who have followed me will also sit on twelve thrones, judging the twelve tribes of Israel. 29 And everyone who has left houses or brothers or sisters or father or mother or children or fields, for my name's sake, will receive a hundredfold, and will inherit eternal life. 30 But many who are first will be last, and the last will be first.

Matthew 19:16-30, NRSV

Have one person in your group read the passage aloud. Have others read silently from different versions. Report any differences in the wording.

Read also how other Gospel writers report this event in Mark 10:17-31 and Luke 18:18-30.

• How does knowing that the rich man is young add to the meaning of this story?
• What questions do differences in translations or other Gospel versions of the story raise for you?

Make a list of the characters in this story. Write the list on a markerboard or large sheet of paper so that everyone can see it. Beside each character's name write words that the group believes describe that character's emotions as the story unfolds.

Invite volunteers to stage brief skits of these conversations:

❑ Jesus and the rich young man (verses 16-22)
❑ Jesus and the disciples (verses 23-30)

• What new insights did the skits provide about the story, Jesus' personality, and the emotions of the characters?
• What do you think motivated the rich young man to come forward? Hope for praise from Jesus? Sincere desire to follow Christ? Both?

3

Following Jesus

4

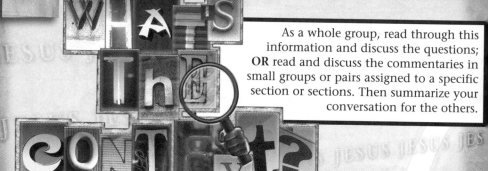

As a whole group, read through this information and discuss the questions; **OR** read and discuss the commentaries in small groups or pairs assigned to a specific section or sections. Then summarize your conversation for the others.

Keep the Commandments

Jesus tells the young man he must "keep the commandments" if he wishes to enjoy eternal life. For the Jewish people, keeping the Ten Commandments meant practicing an obedient way of life that would ensure that they were in right relationship with God and one another.

Review the commandments Jesus mentions in the text. Did you notice that one of them is not among the Ten Commandments? Here, Jesus quotes from the Book of Leviticus (19:18). Read what Jesus has to say about this commandment in Matthew 22:34-40, when he again quotes Leviticus as well as Deuteronomy 6:5. Then go back and read the Ten Commandments (Exodus 20:12-16).

• Which commandments does Jesus say are most important? Why?
• How does the young man's wealth relate to keeping the greatest commandment?
• How does it relate to loving his neighbor?
• Why does Jesus ask the man to give up his possessions? What does the man's response reveal about him?

Read Romans 13:8-10 and Galatians 5:13-14 to see how Paul addresses this subject. Then read Micah 6:8.

• How do these add to your understanding of what it means to keep the commandments?

Matthew's Moses

Jesus is commonly described as the "Moses of the Book of Matthew." Jewish-Christian readers of this Gospel would have noticed several parallels between Moses and Jesus. For example, Moses receives the Ten Commandments upon a mountain; Jesus explains during a sermon delivered from a mountain what it really means to live under God's law. Review Matthew 5:18-48.

- What new standards does Jesus introduce concerning the Ten Commandments?
- Do these standards change the law? Explain.
- How do they raise the standard for obedience to God?

The Synoptic Gospels

Matthew, Mark, and Luke are known as the Synoptic Gospels because they share common stories. *Synoptic* means "seen together." Scholars believe that Mark was the first Gospel to be written and that the writers of Matthew and Luke drew heavily (although not exclusively) upon Mark. You'll find the story of the rich young man/ruler in all three synoptic Gospels. Each writer, however, includes some details that the others omit.

Carefully review both Mark 10:17-31 and Luke 18:18-30.

- List the differences you find in each story.
- Note also what comes before and after this story in each Gospel narrative. How does the placement of the story affect its impact and meaning?

Reread Mark 10:21. Only here is the reporting of Jesus' feelings.

- What reasons do you think were behind Jesus' emotion?
- How does this detail, missing from Matthew and Luke, add to your understanding of Jesus? of the rich young man?

5

6

What Does Money Have to Do With It?

After the young man walks away disappointed, Jesus imposes what sounds like a ridiculously impossible standard. Some scholars believe that his reference to the eye of a needle was a portal, or a small opening in a gate. A camel would have a very, very tight squeeze.

Regardless, Jesus' point remains—and the disciples are as astounded as the rest of the crowd. After all, a rich person was thought to have special favor with God; wealth was supposedly a sign of God's favor. But Jesus stands this traditional belief on its head. Not only is money not enough; it can be a serious obstacle.

- No one in the story asks Jesus the obvious question: Why is it so hard for a wealthy person to enter God's kingdom? How would you answer that question? What does the answer reveal about the kingdom of God?
- Can someone follow all the commandments and still not be in right relationship with God? Explain.
- Why do you think Jesus specifies that the rich young man must give his wealth to the poor, instead of to anyone he chooses? What does this say about following Jesus?
- How does Peter's question regarding what he'll receive for following Jesus relate to Jesus' "eye of a needle" illustration?
- Now address the disciples' question: How can anyone follow such a difficult Gospel?
- Speculate on what you think happened to the rich young man.

With God All Things Are Possible

At first, Jesus' answer to the disciples' question, "Who can be saved?" seems almost flippant, a non-answer. But look deeper. The disciples had already seen Jesus perform many miracles of healing. He calmed the sea before their eyes. He fed a crowd of 5,000. He had been on a mountain with Moses and Elijah.

Read three miracle stories from Matthew: 8:5-13; 9:19-22; and 9:27-30.

- What, according to Jesus, made each miracle possible?
- How does this relate to Jesus' answer to the disciples' question?
- How does it relate to what Jesus demands of the rich young man?
- How has God helped you have more faith?

8

After Looking at Both the Text and the Context...

> **Deal with some or all of these questions before moving to What's Next?**

- What new insights do you have?

- What do you admire about the rich young man? What do you not admire? What traits of his do you see in yourself?

- In what ways do you identify with the rich young man? with Peter and the disciples? with Jesus?

- What does this text say about wealth?

- How does this Scripture help you better understand the Ten Commandments?

- How does God make things easier for us?

- What learning from this text will you apply to your life?

Choose one or more of Views A, B, and C to discuss; **OR** have different small groups talk about one and then summarize the discussion for the other groups. **Be sure to have everyone complete View You.**

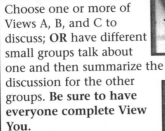

Challenge 1:
Count the Cost

You can see why those who have little might feel freer to follow Jesus than someone like the rich young man. For him, the cost of following Jesus is going to be very high. In the end, he can't bear to pay it.

The Gospels do not tell us that Jesus asked everyone to give up all their possessions. Rather, the story suggests that what really matters is our willingness to follow Jesus, whatever it costs us.

Write down some of the potential costs (not just monetary ones) of following Jesus.

• Which costs would be hardest for you to bear?
• How do the potential costs today compare with those risked by the early followers of Jesus?
• What obstacles might be hindering you from following Jesus more closely?

Some Christians today preach "the Gospel of wealth": that we'll receive financial prosperity as well as treasure in heaven for following Jesus.

• Based on your reading of this text, how would you respond to this Gospel? Why is this Gospel so popular?

Following Jesus

Challenge 2: Give It Up

We know the correct answer to Jesus' challenge. Privately, though, we probably empathize more with the disciples and the rich young man. This teaching is tough—so tough, maybe, that we'd like to conveniently ignore it.

- Can Jesus really be saying that we all must become destitute? Isn't that too hard a standard for a God who recognizes our weaknesses and forgives our sins?
- What is it that Jesus is really asking the rich young man to give up? Is it just the money and possessions?

Think of the trust children place in their parents. When children are small, that trust is complete.

- Why do you think trust in our parents gradually diminishes as we move from early childhood toward adulthood?
- How would you relate this to the rich young man's situation?
- Why is it harder for a rich person than a poor one to put his or her full trust in God?

Challenge 3: Go Last

We're competitive by nature. We want to be chosen before others, to be first in line, to have others look up to us. Jesus consistently teaches just the opposite—and consistently receives a similar reaction from other "haves" as he gets from the rich young ruler. Jesus says that in God's kingdom, "the last shall be first; the first shall be last." God values a humble attitude—letting others go first—more than wealth. The story suggests that accepting this teaching lies at the root of the rich young man's struggle (and ours) to become wholehearted followers of Jesus.

Have one person in your group read aloud the parable of the laborers in the vineyard (Matthew 20:1-16), another story Jesus told to illustrate his point that the first will be last. Talk as a group about these questions:

- How does this parable add to your understanding of Jesus' encounter with the rich young man?
- You can interpret "the last shall be first and the first shall be last" to mean
    —the two will switch places; or
    —"last" and "first" are irrelevant because everyone will be the same.
  Which interpretation would you choose? Why?
- In what ways do you sympathize with the laborers who arrive first? with the landowner? with the laborers who come last?
- In what ways do you practice "going last" as an intentional way of following Jesus? at school? at home? in other circumstances?

following Jesus

12

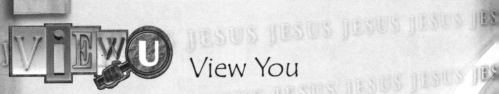

View You

Selling all of his possessions was only the first step in the call Jesus issued to the rich young man. Afterward, the man was to simply follow Jesus—destination unseen, consequences unknown. The second step was perhaps even more difficult than the first. The young man was reluctant to take either step.

Take time to reflect on what God might be calling you to do—in your family, your school, your church, your community—that you are reluctant to do. Consider whether you can make the commitment right now to follow Jesus more deeply.

Write your reflections about this question: How is Jesus calling you into relationship with him?

Check *www.ileadyouth.com/3V*
for worship suggestions.

You Have the Power: Feeding the 5,000

MARK 6:30-44

Have you ever accomplished a task you were certain was impossible? Perhaps you wondered how you would manage it. Maybe you thought (more than once) about quitting. Looking back now, maybe you're still not quite sure how you managed. But you did it.

The disciples received just such an assignment. Fortunately, Jesus was there to show them that, with faith, a little bread can go a long, long way.

13

14

30 The apostles gathered around Jesus and told him all that they had done and taught.

31 He said to them, "Come away to a deserted place all by yourselves and rest a while." For many were coming and going, and they had no leisure even to eat. 32 And they went away in the boat to a deserted place by themselves. 33 Now many saw them going and recognized them, and they hurried there on foot from all the towns and arrived ahead of them. 34 As he went ashore, he saw a great crowd, and he had compassion for them, because they were like sheep without a shepherd; and he began to teach them many things. 35 When it grew late, his disciples came to him and said, "This is a deserted place, and the hour is now very late; 36 send them away so that they may go into the surrounding country and villages and buy something for themselves to eat." 37 But he answered them, "You give them something to eat." They said to him, "Are we to go and buy two hundred denarii worth of bread and give it to them to eat?" 38 And he said to them, "How many loaves have you? Go and see." When they had found out, they said, "Five, and two fish." 39 Then he ordered them to get all the people to sit down in groups on the green grass. 40 So they sat down in groups of hundreds and of fifties. 41 Taking the five loaves and the two fish, he looked up to heaven, and blessed and broke the loaves, and gave them to his disciples to set before the people; and he divided the two fish among them all. 42 And all ate and were filled; 43 and they took up twelve baskets full of broken pieces and of the fish. 44 Those who had eaten the loaves numbered five thousand men.

Mark 6:30-42, NRSV

(Also Matthew 14:13-21; Luke 9:10-17; John 6:1-14)

Have one person in your group read the Bible passage aloud. Have others read silently from different versions and report any differences in the wording.

- How do the differences help you understand the text?

Also read the other Gospel accounts of this event (one of the few recorded by all four Gospel writers) in Matthew 14:13-21; Luke 9:10-17; and John 6:1-14. Then read the story of the feeding of the 4,000 in Matthew 15:32-39 and Mark 8:1-10.

- What differences did you notice among the different Gospel versions of this story? How do these differences add to your understanding of the event? of Jesus?
- What questions does the text raise for you?
- Highlight words or phrases in the text that you feel are important or that raise questions.

Imagine that you are one of the members of the crowd. You have followed Jesus on foot for at least five miles, without knowing when you would return or where you could find something to eat. Why would you do that? What is it about Jesus that has captured your imagination and that of so many others? Write down some of the reasons you think people might have followed Jesus. Compare your answers with those of others in your group.

Following Jesus

16

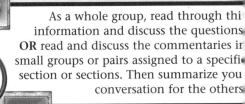

WHAT'S THE CONTEXT?

As a whole group, read through thi
information and discuss the questions
OR read and discuss the commentaries ir
small groups or pairs assigned to a specifi
section or sections. Then summarize you
conversation for the others

Good News

Mark describes his account of Jesus Christ as the "good news," or the *gospel,* of Jesus Christ, the Son of God. (Mark 1:1). Mark was drawing from the Old Testament prophet Isaiah—most notably in a prophecy (Isaiah 61:1) that Jesus said had been fulfilled through him: "The Spirit of the Lord is upon me, because he has anointed me to proclaim good news to the poor" (Luke 4:18a).

To Mark, "good news" was an entirely appropriate description because that is just what Jesus' ministry was, especially to the poor. The religious leaders taught that poverty and disabling conditions were results of sin and that righteous people should have nothing to do with sinners. To be poor or chronically ill was to be cut off from respectability. Yet here was a man who healed the sick, cast out demons from the mentally ill, and announced that people's sins were forgiven. He said that he had come specifically for those who had been lost and cut off from society. And unlike the other teachers, this man spoke like someone who had real authority from God. For people who had little chance and less hope, Jesus was good news for sure!

Read Mark 1:21-28; 1:40-45; and 2:3-12—three stories of healing that Mark places at the beginning of Jesus' ministry.

- How do people react to Jesus?
- How do Jesus' words and actions represent good news?
- How does the message of Jesus represent good news today?

Jesus Christ, Superstar

Imagine the difficulties that movie stars, rock stars, and sports stars encounter when they go out in public. Then you can picture what Jesus faced. Word of his miracles of healing spread like wildfire. Listeners were captivated by his teaching. The crowds grew so large that Jesus avoided going into the towns (Mark 1:45). The disciples were so busy dealing with all of the people who wanted to be healed or to speak to and touch Jesus that they didn't have time even to eat (Mark 3:20 and 6:31).

Hoping for a little peace and quiet, Jesus has the disciples get into a boat and sail across the Sea of Galilee. This "sea" is more like a large lake, about seven miles across at its widest point. John's Gospel says that the deserted place where they landed was near Bethsaida, approximately four miles around the shore from Capernaum, which Jesus often used as a base of operations. People in the crowd, who could see across the lake, guessed where Jesus and the disciples were headed and followed them on foot.

• Why do you think the crowds were so drawn to Jesus?
• How do you think people and the media would react to Jesus today? Why?
• Why does Jesus seek a deserted spot? What does this reveal about Jesus?

Reread the latter part of John's account of the miracle of loaves and fishes (John 6:11-14).

• How does John describe the reaction of the crowd?
• How does Jesus react to their reaction? Why?

17

Following Jesus

18

We Did It?

At the beginning of this text, the disciples return from a "mission trip." Jesus had sent them out in pairs to teach in surrounding villages and had given them authority to cast out demons (Mark 6:7-13). When they return, the disciples tell Jesus about their experiences. We can imagine their excitement as they relate how how the good news had been received and how they had healed sick people and exorcised demons. They had seen God's power working through them, not just through Jesus.

But, as Mark frequently shows, the disciples are slow to understand who Jesus is and what God is doing. When it comes time to feed the multitude, they fall back into a conventional way of thinking. Even after witnessing God's power at work, they don't quite get it.

- Why do you think the disciples react as they do when Jesus tells them to feed the crowd? How would you have reacted?
- What constitutes a miracle? Give some examples of events you would describe as miracles. Why did you view them in this way?
- What does faith have to do with miracles?

Sheep Without a Shepherd

Jesus and the disciples want to rest and recharge and have some quiet time for prayer. Instead, they find another crowd waiting for them as their boat reaches shore.

The disciples are tired and hungry. Had it been up to them, we can imagine that they would have sent the crowds away or headed off elsewhere in the boat. But Jesus—who is just as tired and hungry and just as eager for some peace and quiet—takes a different view.

- Why does Jesus compare the crowd to sheep without a shepherd?
- What does this comparison say about Jesus' understanding of his mission?
- How have you served as a shepherd to someone?

The disciples think that Jesus will certainly agree that their obligation to the crowd has ended when the day grows late. Once again, Jesus leaves them flabbergasted.

- What does this part of the story say about our mission as Jesus' followers?
- At what point in dealing with the poor and hungry do we need to take care of ourselves to avoid burnout and "compassion fatigue"?

Read Luke 10:1-2 (Luke's account, slightly different from Mark's, of the sending out of disciples into towns).

- How does this passage add to your understanding of Jesus' view of the crowds and his refusal to turn them away?

You Feed Them

At times, the disciples must have felt that all of the drudging responsibilities were left to them. Jesus does the "glamorous" work of healing and teaching, while they worry about food and transportation. In their eyes, it's only natural to object when Jesus tells them to feed the crowd. The bread alone would cost 200 denarii. One denarius was the typical pay for an entire day's labor. To feed this whole crowd would cost more than six months' wages. To the disciples, the idea was ridiculous.

- Have you ever had to take on a big responsibility and had no idea how you'd accomplish it? How did you manage? If you were successful, how did that experience affect your willingness to take on other big responsibilities?
- What experiences increased your faith that all things are possible for God?
- How hard is it to live by faith?

Take Time to Relax

Our lives are more hectic than those of any other generation in history. We go from school to sports team practices to piano/guitar/dance lessons to homework to club meetings to service projects. We can relate to the disciples' having little time to grab a meal. We can barely catch our own breath.

When this text opens, Jesus and the disciples are on their way to some much needed rest. Although they don't find it in this case, Jesus recognized the importance of making time for rest and reflection. Along with honoring God, that is why the Sabbath is set apart. Even God needed a day to rest.

- How do you find time to rest?
- What effect does not having enough time to relax in solitude have upon you?
- How important is it for you to get away from the crowds and spend time alone focusing on yourself? Do you have a "deserted place" where you spend time with God?
- What does the Sabbath day mean in your life? In the lives of the people you know?

Following Jesus

After Looking at Both the Text and the Context...

Deal with some or all of these questions before moving to What's Next?

• What new insights do you have?

• With whom did you identify? the crowd? the disciples? Jesus?

• How does this text relate to the good news?

• How important is faith in working miracles?

• What is the role of faith in following Jesus?

• How are faith and trust related?

• What learning will you take from this text and apply to your life?

Choose one or more of Views A, B, and C to discuss; **OR** have different small groups talk about one and then summarize the discussion for the other groups. **Be sure to have everyone complete View You.**

Living by Faith

Imagine the frustration the disciples must have felt with Jesus when he told them to feed 5,000 people. *What was he thinking?* they probably wondered. More to the point, however, is how *they* were thinking. Instead of entrusting the task to God, they viewed it as one they would have to handle with their own resources.

The lesson is one that Jesus taught over and over: To participate in the abundant life God offers, we must live by faith and trust God, for whom nothing—not even feeding a crowd with only a little bread and fish—is impossible.

Read Malachi 3:10, the Word of God spoken through an Old Testament prophet.

• How does this text add to your understanding?
• What does it mean to live by faith?
• How would your life change if you lived completely by faith?
• To what extent should you rely on your own resources and abilities if you are living by faith? Why?

Feeding the Hungry

Famine haunts North Korea and many African nations. Even in America, people go hungry. Providing food for them creates financial and logistical challenges that the disciples could never have imagined. Even the best efforts of professional relief organizations are not enough.

Why does God allow hunger? Maybe the story from Mark teaches that this is the wrong question to ask. Jesus issues the same challenge to us as he gave his disciples: You care for them. Jesus commands us, as followers, to feed the hungry, clothe the naked, welcome strangers, visit those who are imprisoned—and meet their spiritual needs too.

- For what was the crowd that followed Jesus around the Sea of Galilee hungering? In what ways were they fed?
- Why do you think Jesus leaves this responsibility to us?

Read John 21:15-17.

- What does it mean to feed God's sheep?
- Discuss ways in which your group can help those in need in your church, school, community, or around the globe? Draft a plan that your church could implement, or by which your group could assist with an existing effort?
- How will faith play a part in your plan?

VIEW C   Pass the Leftovers

How many times have you heard a parent tell you to clean your plate because people elsewhere were starving? Jesus might have said the same thing. Did you notice that the disciples don't just leave the leftovers on the ground after everyone finishes? They gather the leftovers into baskets. Obviously, they plan to share—and pass on the miracle to others.

We live in a society with abundant resources. American households waste tons of food annually. Besides throwing away food, we throw away paper, glass, metal, and plastic that could be recycled.

• What do you do with your leftovers?
• What do you recycle?

Take time this week to monitor your use of leftovers.

• How can we be better stewards of the resources God gives us?

As a group, create a list of ways you, your families, and your friends could share with others or recycle, rather than throw away.

View You

Jesus told the disciples that they would perform even greater miracles than he had done. But that power was not extended to only the twelve. God's Spirit works through all followers of Jesus. You may never turn five loaves and two fish into a banquet, but you have power from God to reach out to a world that is hungering to be fed in body and soul.

- How will you recognize that power?
- How will you use it?

In this space or on a separate sheet of paper, write how you can use the power that God gives you:

To heal

To teach

To feed and nurture

To rebuke demons and confront evil

To spread the Good News

To be a good steward

Check **www.ileadyouth.com/3V**
for worship suggestions.

Caught in the Act

JOHN 7:53—8:11

It's embarrassing to be caught in the act of doing something wrong. We feel ashamed. We feel disapproval, even condemnation, from others. But Jesus showed that this worst-case scenario can be one of the best things ever to happen to us (and to our accusers).

27

28

53 Then each of them went home, 1 while Jesus went to the Mount of Olives. 2 Early in the morning he came again to the temple. All the people came to him; and he sat down and began to teach them. 3 The scribes and the Pharisees brought a woman who had been caught in adultery; and making her stand before all of them, 4 they said to him, "Teacher, this woman was caught in the very act of adultery. 5 Now in the law Moses commanded us to stone such women. Now what do you say?" 6 They said this to test him, so that they might have some charge to bring against him. Jesus bent down and wrote with his finger on the ground. 7 When they kept on questioning him, he straightened up and said to them, "Let anyone among you who is without sin be the first to throw a stone at her." 8 And once again he bent down and wrote on the ground. 9 When they heard it, they went away, one by one, beginning with the elders; and Jesus was left alone with the woman standing before him. 10 Jesus straightened up and said to her, "Woman, where are they? Has no one condemned you?" 11 She said, "No one, sir." And Jesus said, "Neither do I condemn you. Go your way, and from now on do not sin again."

John 7:53–8:11, NRSV

Have one person in your group read the Bible passage aloud. Have others read silently from different versions and report any differences in the wording.

• How do the differences help you understand the text?
• What questions do the differences raise for you?

Highlight words or phrases in the text you feel are important. Make a list of questions the text raises for you.

Invite volunteers to dramatize this story, using a different set of facts: Some "teachers' pet" students in your school have caught a fellow student in the act of cheating on a test. They have brought this person to the principal. The school's strict policies clearly state that cheaters will be expelled and receive a failing grade.

• What stood out in seeing the story from a different perspective that you did not think about earlier?
• How did your understanding of the story change?
• What new questions does this experience with the text raise for you?
• How does this text relate to following Jesus?

Add the new highlights and questions to the list.

following Jesus

30

WHAT'S THE CONTEXT?

As a whole group, read through this information and discuss the questions; **OR** read and discuss the commentaries in small groups or pairs assigned to a specific section or sections. Then summarize your conversation for the others.

Jesus and the Law

The seventh commandment says, "You shall not commit adultery." The Law handed down from the time of Moses (and strictly followed by the Pharisees) was equally clear: "If a man commits adultery with the wife of his neighbor, both the adulterer and the adulteress shall be put to death" (Leviticus 20:10).

Stoning was the form of execution used by the people of Judea (crucifixion was reserved for use by Roman authorities). Angered by Jesus' influence over the people, the Pharisees and scribes plotted against Jesus. Although the Romans allowed the Jewish people to practice their religion, they would not permit them to execute people for violations of Jewish religious laws. (That's why the religious leaders who wanted to kill Jesus took him to Pilate, the Roman governor.)

Jesus preached a different understanding of Jewish Law and came into conflict with the religious leaders. To Jesus, the Pharisees and scribes had become so preoccupied with the letter of the Law that they were missing the more important spirit of the Law—the emphasis on forgiveness and mercy as much as obedience.

- Where have you seen people more concerned with the letter of the law than the law's spirit? or using the law for their own ends? or applying the law in some cases and not others?
- Why were the Pharisees so concerned about following the letter of the Law?
- When do you think it's more important to follow the spirit of the law than the letter? to follow the letter?

Jesus and the Pharisees

The Pharisees were religious teachers who believed that the key to God's favor was strict obedience to the hundreds of detailed requirements in law code of Moses. Pharisees were popular with the people, in part because of their opposition to the elite priestly class known as the Sadducees. The scribes (sometimes termed "lawyers" in the Bible) interpreted and kept the Torah Law. These three groups are often mentioned in the Scriptures in opposition to Jesus.

John records that many Pharisees believed that Jesus could not have worked miracles of healing unless he had authority from God. But most members of the Jewish religious leadership opposed Jesus' ministry. They believed that God would send a Messiah to liberate the Jewish people and save the world, yet they also believed that anyone who claimed to *be* that Messiah (as others had before Jesus) was a blasphemer (someone who mocked God).

The oppressive occupation of their land by Rome moved the Jewish religious leaders to cling even more to obeying the Torah Law, in hope of receiving deliverance. When Jesus appeared, forgiving sins (reserved for God alone) and preaching a new understanding of the Mosaic Law, he gained a huge following. At times, Jesus condemned the Pharisees and scribes as hypocrites who cared more about outward shows of religion than about having a pure heart (see Matthew 23). Before we meet the woman caught in adultery, the tension between Jesus and the religious leaders had escalated to the point where they were plotting to kill Jesus.

- Where do you see people today who are caught up in observing the law, as were the Pharisees?
- Why were Jesus and the Jewish religious rulers opposed to one another? Why do you think the Pharisees were plotting against Jesus and wanted to kill him?

A Set-up and a Pawn

The woman caught in adultery is also caught in the middle of Jesus' conflict with the Pharisees. While he is teaching, they send the Temple police to arrest him. When the police arrive, Jesus continues to teach and describes himself as "living water." The police listen but take no action. "Why haven't you arrested him?" the Pharisees demand. The awestruck police respond, "Never has anyone spoken like this." (Check out the story in John 7:32-47.)

After this failed attempt to stop Jesus, some Pharisees devise a plan to trap Jesus. As Jesus teaches in the Temple early the next morning, they pull the woman into the middle of the crowd. Never mentioning her partner's sin, they focus only on the woman's guilt. Executing her is beside the point (they know they can't kill her without Roman permission); the real aim is to draw Jesus into a debate over the Torah Law concerning adultery and hope that he will make a public statement they can use against him. The woman is merely a pawn in their game.

If Jesus disagrees that the woman should be stoned, he would contradict Torah Law; if he endorses stoning, the Pharisees could say that Jesus advocated violating Roman rules.

- How does Jesus respond to the Pharisees' question?
- Why do you think Jesus draws in the sand while the Pharisees speak?
- What do the actions of religious leaders say about their relationship with God?
- How does Jesus make this conversation with his opponents peaceful?
- How does his response influence the outcome of the story? Had he responded differently, how might the outcome have changed?
- How does Jesus' response provide an example for us?

From Guilt to Grace

This story brings into sharp contrast the differing ways that Jesus and the Pharisees view sin. To the Pharisees, who are obsessed with following the exact letter of the Torah Law, faithful people should avoid contact with sinners, lest they also fall into sin. Additionally, in the Pharisees' way of thinking, some sins (such as adultery) are so abhorrent to God that they warrant the ultimate punishment; repentance is out of the question.

Jesus preaches a radically different message: "God did not send the Son into the world to condemn the world, but in order that the world might be saved through him" (John 3:17). Jesus came to bring sinners back into a right relationship with a loving God, not to foreclose all hope of their repentance. Salvation is not something we imperfect humans can earn on our own through obedience and sacrifices of atonement; salvation is God's generous gift to everyone who will embrace it. God brings us from guilt to grace.

No wonder Jesus and the religious leaders are in conflict. They completely disagree over the most fundamental questions of God's nature and purposes.

Read or recall the parable of the laborers in the vineyard (Matthew 20:1-16).

• How does this story also help you understand the idea of God's grace?

33

Guilty Silences

As the old saying goes, "Silence gives consent." Significantly, the woman brought before Jesus remains silent while the Pharisees accuse her. Perhaps she does not dispute the charge because, as the religious leaders claim, she was caught in the very act. In this case, her silence may be an acknowledgment of her guilt and shame.

Then, when Jesus turns the tables and forces the Pharisees to examine their own consciences, they suddenly grow silent too. From the way John relates the story, we understand the Pharisees' silence to mean that they recognize that they are not without sin. They had no right to judge.

- Recall a time that you were guilty and remained silent. Did anyone figure you to be the guilty person because of your silence?
- Why do you think the woman remains silent in the presence of her accusers?

Note the one occasion in this entire episode when the woman speaks (verses 10-11).

- What prompts the woman to speak?
- What might these two verses reveal about the contrasting ways in which the Pharisees and Jesus view the woman?
- What do they say about how God views us?
- How does Jesus turn the woman from being a mere pawn into being a real person?

The Handwriting in the Sand

Jesus does not immediately respond to his opponents' questioning about executing the woman. Nor does he correct their misinterpretation of the Mosaic Law as it related to adultery, which requires *both* the man and the woman to be stoned. Instead, he doodles on the ground. (Some scholars suggest that Jesus wrote the names of the accusers along with their sins.)

- What do you think Jesus is writing? Is it significant to know what or why he is writing?
- Do you think that Jesus is rude to the Pharisees?
- Why do you think the woman remains standing after all of the men drop their stones and leave?
- What does this say about the woman's character? What might her posture say about Jesus?

following Jesus

After Looking at Both the Text and the Context...

Deal with some or all of these questions before moving to What's Next?

- What new insights do you have?

- How do Jesus' actions in this story help us better understand the challenge of following Jesus?

- Are forgiving and being a forgiven prerequisites for discipleship?

- In what ways do we judge others?

- Characterize Jesus' response to the woman in one word. What do you think Jesus' response reveals about the nature of God's kingdom, whose arrival Jesus proclaimed?

- What would you have done had you been in Jesus' position?

- What would you have done had you been in the woman's position?

- What learning from this text will you apply to your own life?

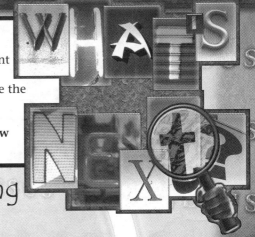

Choose one or more of Views A, B, and C to discuss; **OR** have different small groups talk about one and then summarize the discussion for the other groups. **Be sure to have everyone complete View You.**

Amazing Grace

Notice what seems to matter most to the characters in this story. The Pharisees care about trapping Jesus. The older men in the crowd care about upholding the religious Law, as they understand it. The younger men blindly follow the older men. Only Jesus seems genuinely to care about the woman.

This story carries a powerful message about grace. Following Jesus means participating in this grace and pouring it out upon others. It's not that God doesn't care about sin. It's that God cares more about being reconciled with us than about simply condemning us. And the only way we imperfect humans can be reconciled with God is through God's free gift of grace.

- Do you think that, at the end of the story, the woman becomes a follower of Jesus? Why, or why not?
- Why would a righteous God care more about forgiveness than upholding the rules?
- If God is going to forgive us, why should we worry about sinning?

Before he became a Christian, John Newton captained a ship involved in the trading of African slaves. Later, he wrote the words to one of our most beloved hymns: "Amazing grace, how sweet the sound, that saved a wretch like me."

- How do you think Newton would have related to the woman caught in adultery?
- How does Newton's story add to your understanding of grace?

37

Following Jesus

 Confronting Our Sin

We hate to be caught with our "hand in the cookie jar." We want our sins to remain hidden. That's human nature. But that's not an option for the woman in this story. Her sin is broadcast to the entire crowd. Her shame is extremely public.

Yet this low point in the woman's life also created the opportunity for its high point: meeting Jesus. Being forced to confront her sin provided the means for the woman to experience forgiveness and liberating grace.

At times we need to get caught in our wrongdoings so that we can receive deliverance from the bondage of sin and eliminate the potential of hurting ourselves or others.

- Why is it important to confess your sins?
- How can failing to confront and confess our sins keep us in bondage?
- What risks are involved in exposing our sins?
- How did the woman benefit from the actions of the religious leaders?
- How did she suffer? How did Jesus respond to this suffering?
- When you pray a prayer of confession in worship, what is that experience like for you? How might you view that time differently after this study?

Throwing Stones

Unfortunately, the story of the condemned woman is not a relic of the ancient past. According to recent news reports, a Muslim religious court in Sudan sentenced a woman to death for having an adulterous affair. (A similar case in Nigeria has also drawn worldwide attention.) Although the woman denied the allegation, she could not produce four witnesses to support her theory of the case. Christian relief organizations pressured the Sudanese government to overturn the death sentence. It seems incredible that we could hear of such a story today.

Almost as mind-boggling, perhaps, is that the men involved in the alleged adultery in both the Sudanese and Nigerian cases escaped without arrest, judgment, or public humiliation. Perhaps they—and the other men in John's story of sin— believed that gender, race, economic status, or social rank makes them superior to their own sin. The Pharisees sincerely believed that they were carrying out God's will by judging the adulterous woman. Until Jesus confronted them, they were blind to their own sin.

- How did Jesus extend grace to the men as well as to the adulterous woman in this story?
- How can we confront hypocrisy without condemning persons?
- Where do you think the adulterous man was during this time?
- How does the story of the Sudanese woman compare with the woman in the Bible story? What are the differences? Is Jesus still present?
- What other examples do you know of people who feel superior to others and who are blind to their own sin? Do any of those examples include you?

39

Following Jesus

VIEW U — View You

When others throw stones at us, it hurts. When we condemn ourselves, it can hurt even more. Clench your fist. Imagine that it holds a stone. Now imagine that you're carrying one stone for every sin you've ever committed—and that all of those stones would be thrown at you.

When we carry around the enormous weight of guilt, we cannot easily follow Jesus. When we beat ourselves up with stones of self-condemnation, we cannot experience the joy of Jesus' love in our lives. When we cast stones at others, we deny the possibility of God's healing and restoration. We make it hard to live in community.

Slowly open your hand and "let go" of your stones.

In this space, or on a separate sheet of paper, write your reflections about these questions:

• How is Jesus strengthening me to release the stones I carry?
• How does the act of releasing my stones make me free?
• What is God calling me to do in response to this Word?

Check *www.ileadyouth.com/3V*
for worship suggestions.

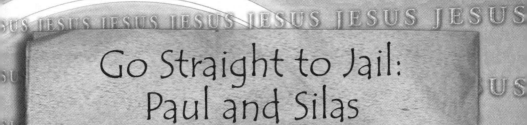

Go Straight to Jail: Paul and Silas

ACTS 16:16-39

Have you ever suffered for doing the right thing? Paul and Silas could relate. They helped a young woman in distress and then found themselves in jail. Jesus warned that there'd be days like this.

42

16 One day, as we were going to the place of prayer, we met a slave girl who had a spirit of divination and brought her owners a great deal of money by fortune-telling. 17 While she followed Paul and us, she would cry out, "These men are slaves of the Most High God, who proclaim to you a way of salvation." 18 She kept doing this for many days. But Paul, very much annoyed, turned and said to the spirit, "I order you in the name of Jesus Christ to come out of her." And it came out that very hour.

19 But when her owners saw that their hope of making money was gone, they seized Paul and Silas and dragged them into the marketplace before the authorities. 20 When they had brought them before the magistrates, they said, "These men are disturbing our city; they are Jews 21 and are advocating customs that are not lawful for us as Romans to adopt or observe." 22 The crowd joined in attacking them, and the magistrates had them stripped of their clothing and ordered them to be beaten with rods. 23 After they had given them a severe flogging, they threw them into prison and ordered the jailer to keep them securely. 24 Following these instructions, he put them in the innermost cell and fastened their feet in the stocks.

25 About midnight Paul and Silas were praying and singing hymns to God, and the prisoners were listening to them. 26 Suddenly there was an earthquake, so violent that the foundations of the prison were shaken; and immediately all the doors were opened and everyone's chains were unfastened. 27 When the jailer woke up and saw the prison doors wide open, he drew his sword and was about to kill himself, since he supposed that the prisoners had escaped. 28 But Paul shouted in a loud voice, saying, "Do not harm yourself, for we are all here." 29 The jailer called for lights, and rushing in, he fell down trembling before Paul and Silas. 30 Then he brought them outside and said, "Sirs, what must I do to

be saved?" *31* They answered, "Believe on the Lord Jesus, and you will be saved, you and your household." *32* They spoke the word of the Lord to him and to all who were in his house. *33* At the same hour of the night he took them and washed their wounds; then he and his entire family were baptized without delay. *34* He brought them up into the house and set food before them; and he and his entire household rejoiced that he had become a believer in God.

35 When morning came, the magistrates sent the police, saying, "Let those men go." *36* And the jailer reported the message to Paul, saying, "The magistrates sent word to let you go; therefore come out now and go in peace." *37* But Paul replied, "They have beaten us in public, uncondemned, men who are Roman citizens, and have thrown us into prison; and now they are going to discharge us in secret? Certainly not! Let them come and take us out themselves." *38* The police reported these words to the magistrates, and they were afraid when they heard that they were Roman citizens; *39* so they came and apologized to them. And they took them out and asked them to leave the city.

Acts 16:16-39, NRSV

Have one person in your group read the Bible passage aloud. Have others read silently from different versions and report any differences in the wording.

• How do the differences help you understand the text?
• What questions do the differences raise for you?

Highlight words or phrases in the text that you feel are important. Make a list of questions the text raises for you.

Invite volunteers to act out Paul and Silas's encounter with the fortune-teller and their prison experience.

• What stood out as you watched the story that you didn't think about earlier?
• What questions arise for you after this experience with the text?

Add the new highlights and questions to the list.

43

Following Jesus

44

WHAT'S THE CONTEXT?

Church Growth

As a whole group, read through th[e] information and discuss the question[s] **OR** read and discuss the commentaries i[n] small groups or pairs assigned to a specifi[c] section or sections. Then summarize you[r] conversation for the other[s].

Acts tells the story of two distinct movements among the followers of Jesus. One, led by Peter, consisted of Jewish Christians. They stressed the importance of keeping the Jewish dietary codes, cleansing rituals, and circumcision. The other, led by Paul, focused on converting the Gentiles. Paul believed that Gentile Christians needed not to practice Jewish rituals; to Paul, salvation came through faith in Jesus alone. Disagreements arose between the two movements, and between Paul and Peter, over this issue. Paul's letter to the Galatians, for example, is a spirited plea with these Gentile Christians not to listen to teachers who claimed that the Galatians must live under Jewish religious laws.

Had Paul's interpretation not ultimately prevailed, Christianity might have remained only a sect within Judaism. During the period of Paul's journeys (A.D. 46–57), Christianity was widely perceived as just that. Undoubtedly, this perception was encouraged by Paul's own actions. When he first visited a city, Paul often began by teaching in the local synagogue. In Philippi, the setting for this text, there was no formal synagogue, so Jews gathered by the river for the Sabbath. That is where Paul and Silas were headed when they met the fortune-telling slave girl.

- How might Christianity be different today if Paul's views had not been adopted?
- Why do you think many Jewish Christians insisted that Gentile Christians observe Jewish laws and rituals?

Who Are Paul and Silas?

We first meet Paul (then known as Saul) in Acts 7, at the stoning of Stephen in Jerusalem. Luke tells us that Saul approves of killing Stephen (Luke 8:1). Paul is a member of the Hebrew tribe of Benjamin and persecutes Christians zealously (Philippians 3). On his way to arrest disciples of Jesus, Saul encounters Jesus Christ himself on the Damascus Road. Knocked off his horse and blinded for three days, Paul is transformed from one of the greatest persecutors of Christians to the greatest Christian missionary. Paul ultimately makes three long missionary journeys before his final trip to Rome. Everywhere he goes, he wins new followers for Jesus. Almost everywhere, too, he meets persecution—in the form of beatings; lashings; imprisonment; and, ultimately, death.

We know much less about Silas. We first meet him when the church in Jerusalem sends him as an envoy to the Gentile Christians in Antioch (Acts 15:22-29). Paul chooses Silas as his partner to accompany him on his second missionary journey across what is now Turkey. Led by the Holy Spirit, they cross the Aegean Sea into Europe and preach at Philippi, where they are arrested. Later, they travel along the Greek coast to Thessalonica and Berea; their preaching causes riots in both places (Acts 17:1-13). They work separately for a time then meet in Corinth (Acts 18:5). Luke does not mention Silas (known to the Corinthians by a Greek rendering of his name, Silvanus) again.

- What do you think about Paul's decision to follow Jesus?
- What does God's choice of Paul say about God?
- Do you think that we choose to follow Jesus, or does he choose us? Explain.
- Although the Bible says very little about Silas, what type of person do you think he was? What qualities would he have had that made Paul want him as a partner?

Following Jesus

Jailed for Healing?

On their way to prayer in Philippi, Paul and Silas meet a slave girl, who has a spirit of "divination." The slave girl is a "Pythoness," that is, she is possessed by the spirit of a mythical python that Greeks believed guarded the fortune-telling Oracle of Delphi. People paid large amounts of money to consult with these fortunetellers.

Casting out a spirit, as Paul does, is no crime. So the owners tell the magistrates that Silas and Paul are Jews who are stirring up trouble. *That* is a legal problem.

For one thing, it was illegal for Jews to make converts of Romans, as the slave-owners accuse Paul and Silas of doing (Acts 16:21). For another, the magistrates have the duty of keeping order. The magistrates also would have to have been aware that the Emperor Claudius had recently expelled Jews from Rome as troublemakers.

• Why are the girl's owners angry with Paul?
• How do you think the slave girl feels?
• Can you do the right thing and still break a rule? Which is more important? Is it always more important?
• How do the authorities respond to the charges against Paul and Silas?
• How do you think Silas feels about being arrested, especially since he is only a bystander when Paul casts out the spirit?

A Double Standard

Did you notice how Paul says one thing that changes everything? When the magistrates hear that Paul and Silas are Roman citizens, the magistrates suddenly become both afraid and apologetic—and with good reason.

It was illegal to flog a Roman citizen without a hearing (or what we today call "due process"). Three Roman acts of law—*Lex Valeria, Lex Porcia*, and *Lex Julia*—protected Roman citizens, who could be beaten only if they refused to obey a magistrate's orders or had been formally convicted of wrongdoing. Even after a conviction, citizens enjoyed the right to an appeal. In the case of Paul and Silas, the magistrates realize that they have violated Roman law and can be severely punished if these citizen-apostles complain to higher authorities.

Notice one other thing too. These rights apply *only* to Roman citizens, who gained their status by birth or by having enough wealth to purchase it. Everyone else is out of luck.

- How would the case of Paul and Silas be handled in present-day America?
- Why do you think Paul and Silas choose not to mention their Roman citizenship until after they have been freed to leave?
- How does your understanding of the legal double standard for citizens and non-citizens help you appreciate the appeal of Paul's teaching that all believers enjoy equality in Christ? How might that teaching have helped fuel the growth of the church?
- Do double standards exist today in the way our laws are administered? If so, where?

After Looking at Both the Text and the Context . . .

Deal with some or all of these questions before moving to What's Next?

- What new insights do you have?

- What stands out to you in the story now?

- What answers have you gained to questions you raised earlier?

- Make a list of the different characters in the story. Beside each character's name, write a word that describes him or her.

- In what ways can you identify with any of these characters?

- Have you ever been unfairly punished? Has anyone ever challenged your innocence? How did you react?

- What learning will you take from this text and apply to your own life?

Choose one or more of Views A, B, and C to discuss; **OR** have different small groups talk about one and then summarize the discussion for the other groups. **Be sure to have everyone complete View You.**

Rejoice

Have you ever heard the saying "No good deed goes unpunished?" Following Jesus can often lead us to places that we never thought we would be, including prison. Many Christians around the world still face the possibility of persecution, or even death, for daring to follow Jesus. Even amid our freedom, we may be ridiculed or isolated for our faith. We may be mistreated for doing the right thing.

Paul and Silas had a simple response to persecution: Rejoice! In jail, they sang. They continued praying. They praised God, in spite of all they had endured.

- How can they (and we) possibly rejoice when things seem at their worst?
- What does faith have to do with it?

Read Philippians 4:4-7, from a letter that Paul wrote to the Christians in Philippi more than a decade after his first visit.

- How does rejoicing and praising God in all situations bring peace "that surpasses all understanding"?
- How do Paul's words echo those of Jesus in Luke 12:22-31?
- In what ways can you can rejoice in suffering?

Following Jesus

VIEW B Fools for Christ

In his first letter to the believers at Corinth, Paul writes that he is a fool for Christ's sake (1 Corinthians 4:10) because God has "made foolish the wisdom of the world" (1:20). How right that must have seemed to those who shared the jail with Paul and Silas that night!

Down in the prison's innermost cell, Paul and Silas, who must still be in great pain from being whipped, don't despair or complain. Instead, they sing and pray so loudly that all of the other inmates can hear them. When the earthquake loosens their chains and provides a means of escape, Paul and Silas stay put (and, perhaps, persuade the other prisoners to remain).

Praising God in spite of beatings and imprisonment is a powerful witness to their faith, and it no doubt makes an impression on those around them. It may seem crazy to remain in their cell when they can flee. But their actions indicate that Paul and Silas put their trust in God, not fate—and those actions make all the difference to the jailer and his family.

- Why do you think the jailer wants to be baptized when he finds that Paul and Silas are still in their cells?
- What impression do you think Paul and Silas make on the other prisoners?
- In what ways does God make the wisdom of the world seem foolish? How has God made what seemed to the world like foolishness into wisdom?
- In what ways have you ever been viewed by others as a fool for Christ?

 A Liberating
Experience

Notice the ways in which this story revolves around freedom and imprisonment. Obviously, it's about the imprisonment and release of Paul and Silas. In her own way, however, the slave girl is captive too. Her owners apparently don't care about her as a person; they're concerned only with her fortune-telling ability. The jailer is also a prisoner. An earthquake in the middle of the night is beyond his control, yet he still must pay with his life if his prisoners escape.

- In what ways is the slave girl liberated?
- What does it say about Paul that he chose to cast out the "spirit of divination"? What does it say about Paul's view of women? about the nature of Christianity and the early church?
- In what ways was the girl's fortune-telling ability both a benefit and a curse?
- In what ways was the jailer saved? the jailer's family?
- Put yourself in the jailer's place. What would be your impression of Christianity, based on your experience with Paul and Silas in the prison?
- Think of persons you know who need to be "liberated" from something that controls them. How could this story speak to their situations?

Read Luke 8:27-35 and compare these stories to Paul's encounter with the slave girl.

- What new insights do you have about this story?

51

 View You

Read Romans 8:28. Think about how Paul's words apply to this story. How, for example, does God use the terrible whipping and imprisonment of Paul and Silas to work for good?

Now read Philippians 1:12-14. These are words that Paul wrote to his friends in Macedonia (among them, perhaps, the jailer and his family) while he was a prisoner in Rome. How do these verses add to your understanding?

In this space or on a separate sheet of paper, write your answers to these questions:

• What kind of faith does it take to believe that God can work for good in all things?
• How can such faith be liberating? How can it change your life?
• In what ways that may not seem apparent now could God be working through you to accomplish good? How does that make you feel?
• How is God speaking to you through this Word?

Check *www.ileadyouth.com/3V* for worship suggestions.

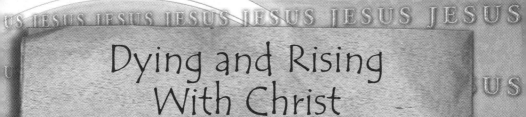

Dying and Rising With Christ

ROMANS 6:1-20

For Christians, the butterfly is a symbol of the Resurrection. But it also can help us understand what happens while we're alive, not just what we experience after our physical bodies die. During its life, the butterfly changes into a completely new creature. It enters the cocoon as a crawling caterpillar and emerges as a beautiful butterfly, with wings that can take it places no caterpillar could ever reach. That, says Paul, is what happens when we become true followers of Jesus.

53

54

1 What then are we to say? Should we continue in sin in order that grace may abound? 2 By no means! How can we who died to sin go on living in it? 3 Do you not know that all of us who have been baptized into Christ Jesus were baptized into his death? 4 Therefore we have been buried with him by baptism into death, so that, just as Christ was raised from the dead by the glory of the Father, so we too might walk in newness of life.

5 For if we have been united with him in a death like his, we will certainly be united with him in a resurrection like his. 6 We know that our old self was crucified with him so that the body of sin might be destroyed, and we might no longer be enslaved to sin. 7 For whoever has died is freed from sin. 8 But if we have died with Christ, we believe that we will also live with him. 9 We know that Christ, being raised from the dead, will never die again; death no longer has dominion over him. 10 The death he died, he died to sin, once for all; but the life he lives, he lives to God. 11 So you also must consider yourselves dead to sin and alive to God in Christ Jesus.

12 Therefore, do not let sin exercise dominion in your mortal bodies, to make you obey their passions. 13 No longer present your members to sin as instruments of wickedness, but present yourselves to God as those who have been brought from death to life, and present your members to God as instruments of righteousness. 14 For sin will have no dominion over you, since you are not under law but under grace.

Romans 6:1-14, NRSV

Have one person in your group read the Bible passage aloud. As a group, list words, phrases, or ideas that stand out.

Then divide into smaller groups. Within the small groups, discuss your understanding of this text. If you wish, rewrite the passage in your own words. Imagine that you've been asked to explain this text to someone at school. Have one spokesperson present to the class what the group believes Paul is saying.

• What new insights did you gain?

Now, have others read this text aloud from one or more translations that use contemporary English. Report any differences in the wording.

• How do differences help you understand the text?
• What new questions does the text raise for you?

Following Jesus

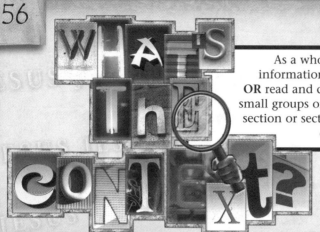

Grace
Happens

As a whole group, read through th
information and discuss the question
OR read and discuss the commentaries i
small groups or pairs assigned to a specifi
section or sections. Then summarize you
conversation for the other:

Human beings are sinners; we have an innate desire to do what we want to do (sin), instead of what God wants us to do. But Jesus Christ's death and resurrection have provided the opportunity, through forgiveness of our sin, to live in harmony and relationship with God. Because God loves us so much, God has freely given us the means through Jesus to live freed of the power of sin. When we accept that gift, we consider ourselves "dead to sin and alive to God in Christ Jesus" (verse 11).

Grace happens every time we experience the love of Christ in our hearts; it happens when we participate in acts that reflect the grace given to us. The more we experience God's grace, the more we are drawn into relationship with God and the less we are prone to sin—the more grace abounds.

- What is the source of God's grace toward us? Why would God forgive us? What does that say about God?
- How would you define grace?
- How have you experienced the grace of God in your life?
- Grace "happens when we participate in acts that reflect the grace given to us." What do you think that statement means? How would you describe acts that reflect grace? Give some examples.

To the Saints

Paul sent this letter to a church he did not start. Although he had connections in Rome and had maintained relationships with some members of the church, most of the Jewish and Gentile Christians there apparently knew Paul only by reputation. So he wrote a letter of introduction before the visit he intended to make on his way to Spain.

The letter is the most complete statement we have of Paul's complex theology. His aim was to outline sound Christian understandings of salvation and faith. The first eleven chapters are packed with Christian theory, while the remaining four present a practical view of living a Christian life.

Paul addresses this letter "to all God's beloved in Rome, who are called to be saints." Today, we tend to think of saints as perfect people. Paul uses the term to describe all Christian believers, who all are sinners saved by grace. Sinners, writes Paul, become saints, justified in God's eyes, through faith in Jesus Christ, who took away the power of sin over our lives. This is Paul's audience—imperfect people who want to know more about how they can become free from sin and enter into a reconciled, right relationship with a perfect God.

• Name some people you would describe as saints. How was or is their faith evident in their lives?
• Are you a saint?
• Review Romans 5:12-21. How do you understand Jesus' sacrifice for our sins?
• What does it mean to be "justified" before God? Why is justification necessary to have a reconciled relationship with God?
• What role do we play in our own justification?

Gotta Serve Somebody

In the Roman world, approximately one in every four persons was a slave. Paul frequently refers to the concept of slavery in his letters. He tells the Romans that, before Christ, we were all enslaved to sin. By dying for our sins, Jesus broke sin's stranglehold over us. As human beings, we still commit sins; but we're forgiven through God's grace.

But just because Christ freed us from sin, that doesn't mean that we are entirely independent. All humans serve someone (or something). Liberation from slavery to sin, says Paul, frees us to become "slaves of righteousness" (Romans 6:15-19). He often refers to himself as Christ's slave. At first, that sounds like a paradox. How can we be free if we're slaves? Easy, says Paul. Obedience to God frees us to become the creatures God always intended us to be. Living only to satisfy human desires (in other words, being a slave to sin) separates us from God and leads to death. Being a slave to righteousness leads to perfection and true freedom.

- How do you think sin enslaves us? What examples can you give of someone being a slave to sin?
- How does Jesus' sacrifice liberate us?
- What examples can you give of someone who is a "slave of righteousness"? (*Don't name the names of persons in your local community.*) What in his or her actions lets you know this?
- How can complete obedience to God make us free?
- Look up the word *sanctification* (Romans 6:19) in a dictionary. Then write the definition in your own words. How does following Jesus prepare us to be sanctified?

Dying to Sin

Paul had some explaining to do. He preached consistently that we cannot be saved by our own actions. By nature, we are too enslaved to sin to escape by ourselves. Instead, salvation is God's gift to us, through grace.

But if good works don't bring us to God, why worry about doing them at all? If grace is good, then won't we receive more of it if we sin more? Those were questions some of Paul's critics were asking. They thought that his teachings didn't make sense.

So in his letter, Paul seeks to address these issues as he introduces himself to the Christians of Rome. He says that, if we are sincere followers, we become new creatures. Our whole nature changes. We become like butterflies.

Reread verse 10.

- What does Paul mean by saying that Christ died to sin?
- What does Paul say that means for us as followers of Jesus?
- Why does Paul say that we must die like Christ?
- How do you understand the experience of dying to sin?
- In what ways do we experience a resurrection by dying to sin?

Born Again

In John's Gospel, a leading Pharisee, named Nicodemus, meets secretly with Jesus. He is intrigued by what he has heard of Jesus' teaching. But he has trouble understanding what Jesus means (as did many other Pharisees).

Read about Jesus' encounter with Nicodemus in John 3:1-8.

- What does Jesus say?
- What does Jesus mean when he speaks of being born of water and the Spirit?
- What does he mean in saying that "what is born of the Spirit is spirit"?
- How is Paul's message to the Romans similar to Jesus' message to Nicodemus? How is it different?

Read 2 Corinthians 5:17 and Romans 8:9-10.

- How do these passages add to your understanding of what it means to be born again and, as Paul writes, to "walk in newness of life" (Romans 6:4) and be "alive to God in Christ Jesus" (Romans 6:11)?

Go back to the question Paul poses in Romans 6:1: "Should we continue in sin in order that grace may abound?"

- In saying that we become new creations (people born of the Spirit), how is Paul answering that question?

Baptism and New Life

For most Christians today, baptism is a symbol of faith in Jesus, an initiation into the church, a promise by an infant's parents, or a claiming of a person by the church as a child of God. To Paul, however, baptism was much more. It was not only a sacrament; it was a transforming experience.

Review Romans 6:1-14.

• According to Paul, what happens to us when we are baptized?
• How does that help us become followers of Jesus?

Christians practice several different forms of baptism today. In some denominations, the person is immersed in water. Other denominations pour or sprinkle water over the person's head. In the early church, however, new Christians were baptized just as Jesus was baptized by John: by being completely submerged. Knowing this may help you understand the imagery Paul uses when he refers to baptism in this text.

• What do you think Paul means when he writes that, through baptism, we have been "buried with Christ"? What is being buried? What emerges from the water? What has changed?
• Review verses 5-14. How can you rephrase them?
• Review verses 1 and 14. What role does grace play? Why do you think Paul begins this discussion on sin and baptism with grace and ends it with grace?
• How do you think grace and the Holy Spirit are related?

Following Jesus

After Looking
at Both the Text
and the Context...

**Deal with some or all of these questions
before moving to What's Next?**

- What new insights do you have?

- How does this text add to your understanding of what it
means to follow Jesus?

- If we become new creatures in Christ, why do we still sin?

- Is it possible not to sin at all? Do you have the power to
choose?

- What does the phrase "present yourself to God" mean to
you? What are ways you can do that?

- Draw a picture to show what dying and rising with Christ
means to you. Tell your thoughts to the others in your
group.

- What learning will you take from this text and apply to your
own life?

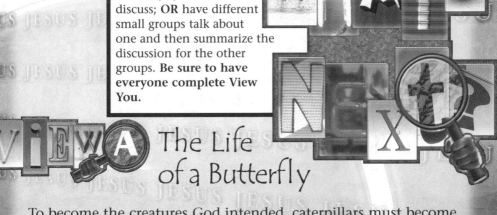

Choose one or more of Views A, B, and C to discuss; **OR** have different small groups talk about one and then summarize the discussion for the other groups. **Be sure to have everyone complete View You.**

VIEW A The Life of a Butterfly

To become the creatures God intended, caterpillars must become butterflies and undergo a dramatic transformation. To realize their true nature, they enter a cocoon and shed their exoskeletons. The old creature dies; and a beautiful, very different one is born. In that same way, we become new creatures in Christ. We are liberated from our old nature, just as the butterfly is no longer bound to crawling as a caterpillar. Unlike the caterpillar, however, we are not capable of becoming new creatures on our own. For us, becoming a "butterfly" is a gift from God that allows us to transcend our own human limitations.

Discuss these questions in small groups:

• What does it mean to be a butterfly in Christ?
• How do the butterfly's entry into and emergence from a cocoon mirror our transformation as Christians? How do they mirror what Jesus went through?
• How does the butterfly's experience help you understand what it means to be baptized and to be in relationship with Jesus Christ?

Answer these questions on your own:

• How are you still transforming? In what stage of the butterfly's life do you see yourself?

63

VIEW B Spiritual Warfare

Paul uses the idea of enslavement to help us understand the power of sin. For people who experience drug, alcohol, smoking, or gambling addictions, enslavement is more than a metaphor; it is very real. Besides these addictions, many people suffer with other kinds of dependency issues. Most carry burdens—just as we carried the burden of sin—that they cannot overcome alone. Fighting addictions is a medical and psychological battle, but it also involves a kind of spiritual warfare.

Read Ephesians 6:10-18. In small groups, discuss these questions:

- How do addictions help you understand the burden of sin? How are they alike? different?
- How do addictions affect the community, our homes, our schools, and the church?
- How can we serve as agents of God's grace in helping people in overcoming addictions?
- What spiritual weapons has God given you in the struggle against "the powers of this present darkness"? What in your faith helps you avoid such enslavements as addictions?
- Do you know someone who has overcome an addiction? How is that person a new creation? What helped him or her?

 Instruments
of Righteousness

Paul says that we are saved by our faith, not by the good works we do. Nevertheless, he quickly adds, if God's Spirit is within us, it will be reflected in the works we do. For that reason, he says, we should give ourselves to God as "instruments of righteousness" (Romans 6:13).

- What is the relationship between the instrument and the one who uses it?
- Using your abilities and resources, how can you be an instrument for God?

Write your answer to the following question on a separate sheet of paper:

- If God were to use you as an instrument of righteousness, what kind of instrument (musical, mechanical, surgical, or other [*name it*]) would you be?

Then fold up your paper and gather everyone's together. Have each member draw one paper that is not his or hers. Talk about each of the images. Come up with more than one answer to these questions:

- Why would this image be a good one for an "instrument of righteousness"?
- What situations need this kind of instrument?

As a group, discuss:

- What does it mean to "present yourself to God" in this way?

following Jesus

ViEWU — View You

Have you ever tried to break a bad habit? You can try to stop "cold turkey," or you can wean yourself from it gradually. Either way, it's hard. Sin is a bit like a bad habit—something we feel compelled to do even when we know it's not good for us. It's our nature. "I do the very things I hate," confesses Paul (Romans 7:15). As Christians, we struggle with our sinful nature, just as Paul did. A bad habit can weigh us down, even enslave us. Knowing that we can never break the "bad habit" of sin is an even heavier burden.

The good news of the gospel, says Paul, is that Christ removed the burden of sin from our lives, once and for all time. What we struggle in vain to accomplish ourselves Jesus has already done for us.

- How does God's gift of grace through Christ make you feel free?
- How does knowing that you have received this gift make you want to respond?
- How does your response reveal that you are a new creation?

Write your reflections about this question:

- How is God speaking to me today through this text?

Check *www.ileadyouth.com/3V*
for worship suggestions.

Behave Yourself!
ROMANS 12:9-21

We know how to behave. We know that it means respecting our elders, following the rules, chewing with our mouths closed—all that stuff. But behavior as a form of "spiritual worship" to God? Huh?

67

9 Let love be genuine; hate what is evil, hold fast to what is good; 10 love one another with mutual affection; outdo one another in showing honor. 11 Do not lag in zeal, be ardent in spirit, serve the Lord. 12 Rejoice in hope, be patient in suffering, persevere in prayer. 13 Contribute to the needs of the saints; extend hospitality to strangers.

14 Bless those who persecute you; bless and do not curse them. 15 Rejoice with those who rejoice, weep with those who weep. 16 Live in harmony with one another; do not be haughty, but associate with the lowly; do not claim to be wiser than you are. 17 Do not repay anyone evil for evil, but take thought for what is noble in the sight of all. 18 If it is possible, so far as it depends on you, live peaceably with all. 19 Beloved, never avenge yourselves, but leave room for the wrath of God; for it is written, "Vengeance is mine, I will repay," says the Lord. 20 No, "if your enemies are hungry, feed them; if they are thirsty, give them something to drink; for by doing this you will heap burning coals on their heads." 21 Do not be overcome by evil, but overcome evil with good.

Romans 12:9-21, NRSV

Have one person in your group read the Bible passage aloud. Have others read silently from different versions and report any differences in the wording.

- How do differences help you understand the text?
- Is the text difficult to understand? Why, or why not?

Divide the large group into small groups. Ask each group to review the text and then to play a game of charades. One member of the small group should silently act out one of the commands from Paul's list, while the other group members attempt to guess which command is being dramatized.

Make a list on a separate sheet of paper of all the things Paul tells us to do and not to do as Christians.

- What questions does each one of these items raise for you?
- Which items on the list seem easiest to do? Which seem most difficult?

Following Jesus

WHAT'S THE CONTEXT?

As a whole group, read through this information and discuss the questions; **OR** read and discuss the commentaries in small groups or pairs assigned to a specific section or sections. Then summarize your conversation for the others.

A Living Sacrifice

Before Paul lists the rules for Christian living in Romans 12:9-21, he starts with a command: "Present your bodies as a living sacrifice, holy and acceptable to God, which is your spiritual worship" (Romans 12:1). You may immediately wonder, "How can I present my body as a sacrifice while I am alive?" You may also ask, "How can the way I live be a form of worship?"

The sacrifices God desires of us are not the same as the Moses' era animal sacrifices that people made to atone for sins. When Jesus died on the cross, he was the sacrifice who atoned for all of our sins. The "living sacrifice" that we make begins with putting our self-focused desires on the altar and choosing, instead, to do the will of God.

- Do we make our living sacrifice *to be* in relationship with God or *because of* our relationship with God?
- How does making a sacrifice require humility?
- What are some ways this week that you have presented yourself as a living sacrifice? How would you describe that sacrifice as act of worship?
- How does the image of presenting your body [self] as a living sacrifice to God help you in your daily living as a Christian?

Paul's Laundry List

Paul's letters typically contain practical advice for daily living as a follower of Jesus. The list in Romans is one of the longest. There appears to be no pattern or ranking of ideas; instead, Paul seems to rattle off these commands as they come to mind. The sentences are short, yet they are packed with meaning.

1. Love sincerely.
2. Hate evil.
3. Hold to the good.
4. Show love for each other.
5. Honor others more than glorifying yourself.
6. Be diligent.
7. Be fervent in spirit.
8. Serve the Lord.
9. Rejoice in hope.
10. Stay faithful during difficult times.
11. Be devoted to prayer.
12. Share with fellow Christians in need.
13. Practice hospitality.
14. Don't curse people who act badly toward you; bless them instead.
15. Rejoice with those who rejoice.
16. Weep with those who weep.
17. Be of the same mind with other Christians; don't let disagreements disrupt your unity.
18. Don't be haughty or stuck up.
19. Associate with the lowly and the unpopular.
20. Don't be conceited.
21. Don't repay evil with evil.
22. Think honorable thoughts.
23. Live peaceably with all (insofar as it is up to you).
24. Don't take revenge; let God worry about that.
25. Show the same generosity to your enemies as you would to your friends; in doing so, you will overcome evil with good.

- Try to come up with four to six categories into which you could group these twenty-five rules for living. Work first in pairs or threes and then as a larger group. See if you can write just a few statements that would be easy to remember that would give guidance for living as a Christian.
- Choose one of the commands on the list and talk about a time when you were able to obey it. What were the results? How did you feel?
- Choose one of these from the list that you will covenant to work on in the next week. Tell one other person in your group and ask for his or her prayers to support you.

Following Jesus

Our Faith and the Treatment of Others

Paul's audience consisted of Jewish Christians and Gentiles. Many Jewish Christians thought less of the Gentile Christians, who did not observe the cleansing and food laws and were not circumcised. Throughout his letter, Paul seeks to eliminate this tension and to bring Jews and Gentiles together as one body in Christ.

Paul explains in Romans and in some of his other letters that Jewish religious rules were no longer the basis for determining our relationship with God. Under the New Covenant, our *faith* justifies us in God's eyes. How we treat others reflects our level of faith.

Use a separate sheet of paper to rewrite verse 16 in your own words.

- How do you understand the verse in the context of your own life?
- What might lead us to look down upon someone, perhaps even our fellow Christians? When have you seen others behave in this way?
- Why don't we want to associate with people who are not popular or whom people call weird?
- What leads us into thinking that we are "wiser than we are"? What are the consequences of this kind of thinking? How does this relate to the tension between the Jewish Christians and Gentile Christians?
- How does living in harmony relate to following Jesus?
- How can people from different backgrounds be in relationship, while affirming their differences? Give some examples.

Bless Those Who Persecute You

Telling someone to love his or her enemies is a lot easier for those who have never faced persecution. For Paul, however, these words to the Romans are not merely an abstract statement of belief. He faced persecution almost everywhere he traveled to spread the gospel. He was jailed, beaten, severely flogged, held under house arrest, and threatened with death. Jewish leaders in various parts of the Roman world and even some fellow Christians attacked his character and spread lies about him. Under the circumstances, we would understand had Paul retaliated against those who had done him wrong. But he did just the opposite. And he offered a practical reason, not just a theological one, for loving our persecutors.

Read Matthew 5:43-48.

- How does Paul's teaching follow Jesus' teaching?
- How is blessing someone who persecutes you an example of offering yourself as a living sacrifice?

Heaping burning coals on someone's head was a punishment for wickedness. However, look at what Paul says is the means of punishment.

- How might an enemy react to such "punishment"?
- Why does Paul believe that loving our enemies is practical advice, not just our duty as followers of Jesus?
- Why, do you think, does part of good behavior require us to bless someone who attacks and harasses us or people we love? How does forgiveness play a role? When you answer this question, think about your own relationship with Jesus.
- What specific action(s) can you take today to overcome evil with good?

By the way, check out Proverbs 25:21-22. Where does your reward come from?

Following Jesus

After Looking
at Both the Text
and the Context...

> **Deal with some or all of these questions
> before moving to What's Next?**

• What new insights do you have?

• What stands out for you in this text?

• How does this text relate to following Jesus?

• What new questions do you have?

• Are these guidelines possible to meet?

• Which one of the twenty-five do you do well? Give an example.

• Which one is difficult for you to follow? Why?

• How would you condense these verses into one sentence?

• What learning will you take from this text and apply to your own life?

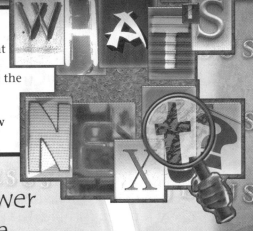

Choose one or more of Views A, B, and C to discuss; **OR** have different small groups talk about one and then summarize the discussion for the other groups. **Be sure to have everyone complete View You.**

VIEW A — The Power of Love

Paul begins this text with love. Although Paul's list of dos and don'ts appears lengthy and disjointed, the items all relate to love. When we decide to do what is loving, we are true followers of Jesus. Paul tells us to love genuinely, with sincerity, and with mutual affection. When we love others, regardless of how they treat us, we have the power to overcome evil.

- Why, in these verses, does Paul seem to focus more on love for people than on love for God? Is it harder to love people and easier to love God? Why?
- Read Romans 12:5. How are Paul's rules for behavior guided by the view expressed in this verse?
- Look at verse 15. When persons are really happy about something special in their life, how easy is it to rejoice with them? Do you ever feel jealous or want to "cut them down"?
- Look at verses 9b and 21. Where would you draw the line between love and hate? How can we hate what is evil, without hating others?
- Have you ever witnessed love overcoming evil? What happened to the person who loved? What happened to the person who did evil?
- How might Paul relate the transforming power of love to Jesus? How might Paul, as a onetime zealous persecutor of Jesus' followers, relate it to his own life?

VIEW B — God, Revenge, and the Death Penalty

After September 11, 2001, many Americans immediately wanted revenge against those who were guilty. In fact, after the attack, Middle Easterners in America experienced hostility because they resembled those responsible for the murders of so many innocent people. The sentiment for revenge still lingers.

Similarly, a majority of Americans say they support the death penalty as a way of promoting justice. Many believe that executing murderers enables victims' families to find closure.

- Why does Paul believe that vengeance belongs to God alone?
- How might God repay?
- Are there times that you have gotten back at someone? What happened? What were the consequences? In looking back, how did you feel at the time? How do you feel about the incident now? What alternatives are you aware of now?
- What were your feelings toward the terrorists after September 11, 2001? How would you apply our text to that situation?
- How does refusing to take vengeance relate to overcoming evil with good?
- When Christians repay an evildoer with evil, what happens to the evildoer? to the Christian? to the church?
- How do you think this text relates to the death penalty?

VIEW C Welcome a Stranger

One Easter morning, a woman walked alone to her church, which was one of the most prominent churches in the city, and encountered a man who emerged from under a bridge. The woman's immediate instinct was to walk faster and ignore the man. Instead, however, she said, "Hello." To her surprise, the man asked whether he could walk with her to church. "Of course," she said. The man hesitated, then confessed, "But the alcohol . . . ?" After taking a smell of his strong odor of alcohol, she responded, "The church is a hospital for sinners."

When the two arrived at the church, there were only two seats left in the back. The man and woman squeezed between two other people. Shortly afterward, a woman on a pew in front of them passed back a peppermint to the man. The man left the church and never returned.

Divide into small groups to discuss the following questions:

- What do you think about the actions of the woman passing the peppermint? Based on your understanding of the text from Romans, what would Paul say about her action?
- How willing are Christians you know to "associate with the lowly"?
- How welcome in your church are the lowly? How can you help make it (even) more welcoming?
- If Michael Jordan or some other celebrity came to your house, would you treat him or her differently than you would a woman wearing rags and smelling of alcohol? Why, or why not?
- If we are truly "members one of another," as Paul says, how would you change your behavior to reflect that belief?

Following Jesus

VIEWU View You

We worship God through our church attendance, our prayers, our songs, and the contribution of our money, time, and energies. But Paul writes of another form of worship, too: worshiping God through the way we live. By living out the items on Paul's list, we are following Jesus and worshiping God.

• Think about your own life. How much are you worshiping God through the way you live?

Read Hosea 6:6, which is a passage quoted by Jesus (Matthew 9:13).

• How does this verse relate to your worship and to Paul's list?

In the space below or on a separate sheet of paper, write your reflections about this question:

• How is God speaking to me today through this text?

Check *www.ileadyouth.com/3V*
for worship suggestions.

Teamwork: Unity of Faith

ACTS 16:16-39

We all like doing our own thing. We like being with persons who think like we do and who like the things we like. We don't like hanging out with persons who don't agree with us. Christians, congregations, and whole denominations are often that way too. Paul has some surprising words for them (and us).

79

¹ I, therefore, the prisoner in the Lord, beg you to lead a life worthy of the calling to which you have been called, ² with all humility and gentleness, with patience, bearing with one another in love, 3 making every effort to maintain the unity of the Spirit in the bond of peace. 4 There is one body and one Spirit, just as you were called to one hope of your calling, 5 one Lord, one faith, one baptism, ⁶ one God and Father of all, who is above all and through all and in all.

7 But each of us was given grace according to the measure of Christ's gift. 8 Therefore it is said:

"When he ascended on high, he made captivity itself a captive;
 he gave gifts to his people."

9 (When it says, "He ascended," what does it mean but that he also descended into the lower parts of the earth? ¹⁰ He who descended is the same one who ascended far above all the heavens, so that he might fill all things.) ¹¹ The gifts he gave were that some would be apostles, some prophets, some evangelists, some pastors and teachers, ¹² to equip the saints for the work of ministry, for building up the body of Christ, ¹³ until all of us come to the unity of the faith and of the knowledge of the Son of God, to maturity, to the measure of the full stature of Christ. ¹⁴ We must no longer be children, tossed to and fro and blown about by every wind of doctrine, by people's trickery, by their craftiness of deceitful scheming. ¹⁵ But speaking the truth in love, we must grow up in every way into him who is the head, into Christ, ¹⁶ from whom the whole body, joined and knit together by every ligament with which it is equipped, as each part is working properly, promotes the body's growth, in building itself up in love.

Ephesians 4:1-16, NRSV

Have one person in your group read the Bible passage aloud. Have others read silently from different versions and report any differences in the wording.

• How do the differences help you understand the text?
• What questions do the differences raise for you?

Highlight words or phrases in the text that seem important or raise questions for you.

• Write down on a separate sheet of paper three issues raised in this text. How do they relate to unity?

Record on your paper how your words or phrases and the issues you highlighted above relate to following Jesus.

• What new questions does this experience with the text raise for you?

Add the new highlights and questions to your list.

following Jesus

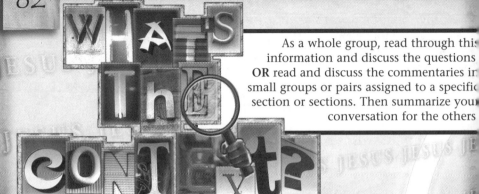

As a whole group, read through this information and discuss the questions OR read and discuss the commentaries in small groups or pairs assigned to a specific section or sections. Then summarize your conversation for the others.

Unity Amid Diversity

Ephesus was one of the largest cities in Asia Minor (modern-day Turkey). Paul spent at least two years of his ministry there, teaching in the Jewish synagogue and, later, in a rented lecture hall. The letter to the Ephesians was probably written a decade later, when Paul was a prisoner awaiting trial in Rome. Some scholars believe that it was a letter that was meant to be distributed to churches throughout the region.

Ephesus was a melting pot of people and religions. There were Greeks, Roman officials, Jews, and others from all over. Many in Ephesus revered the goddess Artemis, whose huge temple was one of the wonders of the ancient world.

In any congregation, creating unity is no easy task. The diversity of the Ephesians made it even more daunting. But Paul's letter still stands as a model for helping Christians maintain a oneness of purpose.

Read the text again. Record the various ways that Paul develops the theme of Christian unity.

• According to Paul, what quality above all joins the body of Christ together? What allows the body to grow?
• What verses illuminate Paul's role as a pastor, or shepherd?

A Recipe for Unity

If you have ever baked a cake or cooked a special dish, you know the importance of following the recipe. (Try making cookies and leaving out the sugar!) In the first few verses of this text, Paul sets forth a recipe for living in unity as Christians. He understood that it is not easy to follow Jesus, to live a life "worthy of the calling to which you have been called." That's why it's important to follow the recipe every day.

Reread verses 1-3. Write down on a separate sheet of paper four key ingredients in Paul's recipe.

• How would you apply these four ingredients to your life?
• What is the body of Christ? (Refer to 1 Corinthians 12:1-31.)
• What is your understanding of the "calling to which you have been called"?
• How does unity relate to that calling?
• Read 1 Corinthians 13. Write down each of Paul's descriptions of Christian love. Match each description with one of the ingredients in Paul's recipe. How do these definitions of love help you understand the ingredients of living in unity?
• What does loving Jesus have to do with loving other people?

following Jesus

Many Gifts, One Body

In several of his letters, Paul uses the metaphor of the human body to explain the nature of the church, which serves as Christ's body on earth. (See also 1 Corinthians 12:1-11 and Romans 12:4-8.) Each part of the human body has a different function, or "gift." So does Christ's body. Just as all parts of the human body must work together for a person to function, the members of Christ's body must work in unity for the church to grow. Each spiritual gift, says Paul, equips the believers for ministry.

List on a separate sheet of paper the gifts within the church (Christ's body) that Paul cites in this text.

- What role does each gift play in the church's growth and ministry?
- Compare the gifts listed by Paul to the roles or "gifts" required for a basketball, baseball, or soccer team. How does each of these athletic gifts relate to the team's overall success?
- What spiritual gifts can you contribute?
- How are you equipped for the "work of ministry"?
- Notice that pastors are only one of the types of persons Paul describes as being in ministry. How do various people in your church serve its ministry?
- How is God calling you to be in ministry?

Speak the Truth in Love

Think of all the influences that can affect how we view ourselves: parents, friends, others at school or work, church, TV, movies, magazines, music. Amid so many often contradictory influences, discerning our gifts and what we believe as Christians may prove challenging. Lots of different, competing ideas sound as if they could hold truth.

The early church was no different. When Paul first visited Ephesus, he found Christians who had never heard of the Holy Spirit. He found non-Christians who called on Jesus' name to cast out demons. He found Apollos, a Jewish Christian preacher from Egypt, whose bold sermons showed little understanding of Christian beliefs. Some Christians taught (much to Paul's dismay) that Gentile followers of Jesus must obey Jewish religious laws. It was hard for the Ephesians to know exactly what to believe. Paul compared the Ephesians to children "blown about by every wind of doctrine."

How should they deal with fellow Christians who disagreed with them over religious teachings? Paul had a recipe for this, too.

• What does it mean to "speak the truth in love"?
• How does Paul's approach help build up Christ's body?
• Which do you think is more important in promoting unity— to speak the truth or to speak the truth in a loving way? Why? Which is more difficult?

If you have time, ask for volunteers to roleplay the skill of speaking the truth in love. Invent a scenario in which one or more students disagree over something. Have one person or group dramatize this argument, while another person or group shows how to disagree in a loving way.

• What new insights did you gain through this exercise?

85

After Looking
at Both the Text
and the Context...

Deal with some or all of these questions
before moving to What's Next?

• What new insights do you have?

• What in the text stands out to you?

• What answers have you gained to the questions you raised
earlier?

• What has this text taught you about being a follower of
Jesus?

• What learning will you take from this text and apply to your
life?

Choose one sentence or phrase from the text and illustrate a
picture to fit it. Show your picture to the others in the group,
and talk about the meaning of it for you.

Choose one or more of Views A, B, and C to discuss; **OR** have different small groups talk about one and then summarize the discussion for the other groups. **Be sure to have everyone complete View You.**

VIEW A

Can We All Get Along?

In the most memorable portion of Dr. Martin Luther King, Jr.'s, famous speech, he spoke of his dream of a world in which people would be judged not by skin color but by character. On that day, he said, the sons of slaves and the sons of slaveholders would hold hands together. "Let freedom ring" would have new meaning. Paul the apostle would have applauded Dr. King, along with the hundreds of thousands of others in front of the Lincoln Memorial on that August day in 1963. After all, Paul had expressed a similar sentiment to the diverse followers of Jesus who made up the early church.

Read Psalm 133.

- How does unity bring freedom?
- How can people who disagree still live in unity?
- How did laws that segregated African Americans from Caucasians in public facilities violate the principles set forth in Ephesians?
- In what other ways do we separate ourselves from others? How do these separations show up in the church? in school? in our communities?
- What roles do forgiveness and spiritual healing play in unity?
- Is it a sin not to live in unity? Why, or why not? How do you think Paul would have answered this question?

87

Following Jesus

VIEW B Playing as a Team

Perhaps you've played on or seen a sports team that had many
talented players yet wasn't very successful. Often, what such a
team lacks is teamwork. Maybe some of the best players hog
the ball or care more about individual success than the team's
success. Sometimes players refuse to work well with those they
don't like. Either way, the "team" has a recipe for failure.

By contrast, when coaches say that a team has "jelled," they
mean that the players all work together unselfishly. These
teams often enjoy more victories than do unharmonious
teams of players with far greater athletic talent. Through a
united effort, a team can accomplish more than the members
can individually—far more than they could have imagined.

- According to Paul, what unites the members of Christ's body
  and makes teamwork possible?
- How is your church or youth group "building itself up in
  love"?
- Are there practices in groups of which you are a part that
  tear down, instead of build up? What might you do to
  change these practices?
- Read Ephesians 3:20-21. How have you seen God work
  through people to accomplish more as a group than they
  could have imagined?

VIEW C Denominational Domination

Jesus' body today is highly fractured. Some of the most bitter religious disputes occur between fellow Christians. Some Christian denominations, believing that theirs is the only true way, refuse to have anything to do with Christians of other denominations. Others believe that members of certain denominations are suspect as Christians because of their affiliation. Even within individual congregations, deep divisions over doctrinal issues lead to splits and the formation of new churches. These days, even more disagreement exists over what it means to be a follower of Jesus than in Paul's time.

- How does Paul's view of the body of Christ allow for religious tolerance and the growth of denominations within the body of Christ?
- How do we "speak the truth in love" to those who disagree with us over points of doctrine, such as infant versus adult baptism or whether Holy Communion should be open to all?
- If different denominations are all part of the body of Christ, why bother to have denominations at all?
- What are the benefits of belonging to a church and to a denomination? Going our separate ways, can we still function as a team in doing the will and work of God?

Following Jesus

View You

Can you imagine hugging a porcupine? It wouldn't be pleasant. Sometimes, when we reach out in love to others, or when we ask their forgiveness, it's like hugging a porcupine. They stick us, and it hurts.

The way to hug a porcupine—carefully, gently, and with love—sounds like Paul's recipe for unity. Reaching out in love puts us at risk; but it is also the only way to experience the forgiveness, reconciliation, and spiritual healing that keep Christ's body functioning as one.

- What "porcupines" have you met? How did you deal with them?
- How does putting yourself at risk bring healing?
- How are you helping to build Christ's body in love?

Take a moment now to pray for the "porcupines" in your life, who react by lashing out. Pray that they will experience the grace of Christ's love and that you will be an agent for healing and reconciliation. Pray also that you will see them differently, not as persons with potential to hurt you, but as persons who need to know God's love. Invite them to be part of Christ's body with you.

Write on a separate sheet of paper your reflections about the following question:

- How is God speaking to me today through this Word?

Check *www.ileadyouth.com/3V*
for worship suggestions.